THE TUNNEL

SHINY

to

My beloved

From

Endless

Contents

I

Dead By Soul

Beginnings are always overwhelmingly joyful and mysterious, but this chapter of my life is mysteriously dark.

I am not me again. This deep void is killing me every moment. I can't even breathe with it, can't feel I'm alive, and feel there is no hope. My heart is shattering every moment. Seeing those broken pieces scattered over the hazy floor, I can't even decide which one to pick up. Instead, I can't decide whether to live or die.

It's bleeding as it has never bled before. In this dark I can't even see the colour of my own blood, I can only scream out of this excruciating pain. This pain does not possess any beauty or strength anymore. I can't bear this pain this time. Screaming inside to meet me again in this lifetime, though my voice is broken, it's very feeble, and no one can hear it.

I feel no moisture of life that will nourish my soul, nothing to restore me back to life. I am becoming very dry from the core of myself, can't feel any pulse of mine. And the alive stream of my life has dried up. Reality has never seemed so cruel before, I'm all choked up. I can only feel my vision is getting blurred. From deep within I can't feel anything anymore, every moment begging to release me from this hell of unknown me.

A room full of unheard silence; those survivor screams are tearing my soul, cutting through my flesh, my veins to taste the blood of my soul. My head is burning, those ashes are colouring my dark canvas.

I do not have the strength anymore after all the fights of this life. This time I'm seeking someone to help me out because I can't even stand on my feet, can't move my lips to utter "SAVE ME! I'M DROWNING."

This corner of the room is also shrinking within me. I can't feel my presence anymore. My existence is getting eliminated from this world in front of my eyes; my eyes can't take it anymore.

This dark is suffocating me, this dark is eating me alive. I felt as if life was baiting me. This darkness promised not to listen to me, not to give me another chance, not to let me live.

Inside this prison, I have caged myself up. This dark I'm cursing, but this pitch darkness of my cracked, shattered soul is the only companion which I could find. This time it's taking my very essence from me. Raindrops from my eyes are asking one question,

THIS ME IS NOT ME! THEN WHO AM I?

Haunting memories deep down the memory lane kept on stabbing me, each and every moment. Dark kept on crawling on my skin. I want to see myself naked, only with my soul. I want to see the blood-covered veins and see my heart beating.

I am numb now, I am eating myself up
I am fragmented and broken down
I am at the edge of my life
Holding onto the dark of unknown me
Believing seems so opaque
Conflicts are screaming so loud
I am possessed by my blurred mind
My demons are pulling me down again
Here my soul goes...

II

A hand (vision of light)

- My eyes never rained before in this way. I could see all of my broken reflections on every drop of my tears. How am I feeling? Why am I feeling in this way? It is a rare scenario that when somebody reaches out to you though you isolated yourself and asks you "How are you?"

Whenever I come across that memory from my past it always gives me chills. I was so scared about the judgements, about the fears which I had, I didn't even have an ounce of courage to go out of my own prison of isolation and ask for help by screaming out loud "I cannot bear the pain anymore, save me." Today when I look back on that phase it seems like a shrinking black hole in the universe that was about to remove her whole existence from this entire world. I will never forget that voice and gesture of kindness, that pat on my back and that question "How are you?" I didn't know what to say. My mind was lying to me; it was so comfortable in that dark hell of isolation that it was raising doubts, conflicts, and thoughts of unknown miseries. I couldn't see the world as it is anymore. I don't know when these delusions became a part of my hazy thoughts, my stalled life.

I can still feel the fragrance of that night. It was 2:45 AM and I was trembling in the cold, I could barely walk with my shivering emotions, this world became a burden to me, I was talking gibberish to myself. From deep within I wanted to feel the warmth of life, I could see myself covered in a grey veil and barbed wires are pricking my flesh, not even sensing the blood which is running through my veins. So cold I am, so vague so infested by the demons of my owned dark.

I was trying to imagine, what a soulful smile feels like? How does it feel to be in peace? Suddenly I encountered that blissful voice and the most unexpected question "are you feeling ok?" Nobody asked about my feelings before, no one asked me this question before! I didn't know that person, still, I don't know his name and names doesn't count when it comes to beautiful souls, souls don't have names, do they

I wanted to say all of it which I was going through but something was holding me back, it's me, my rotten perception about humanity, my own degraded mind, distorted judgements, disintegrated visions, negative projections of my comfortable isolation. All together the fragmented me was unable to share how I was feeling. His words became more generous towards a stranger like me who was looking disoriented at a glance and consoled me to open my heart, still, I question, did a coward like me deserved that humanity, that much of unconditionally? I don't know why my heart felt the need to listen to his warmth of words, but eventually, it did. My heart bleeds on that night like the Nile. My soul was so wounded, I was afraid of everything in fact every feeling of mine.

Afterwards, I realized one thing that when I am not acceptable to myself how am I going to feel accepted by this world? As a human being, I have my own flaws, my own qualities, own capabilities and I function according to those. I am not here on Earth to be perfect neither today have I wanted to be the perfect one. I am unique in my own way. This was the primary realization which I had on that night.

An End is never an end
Every end is the beginning of something new...

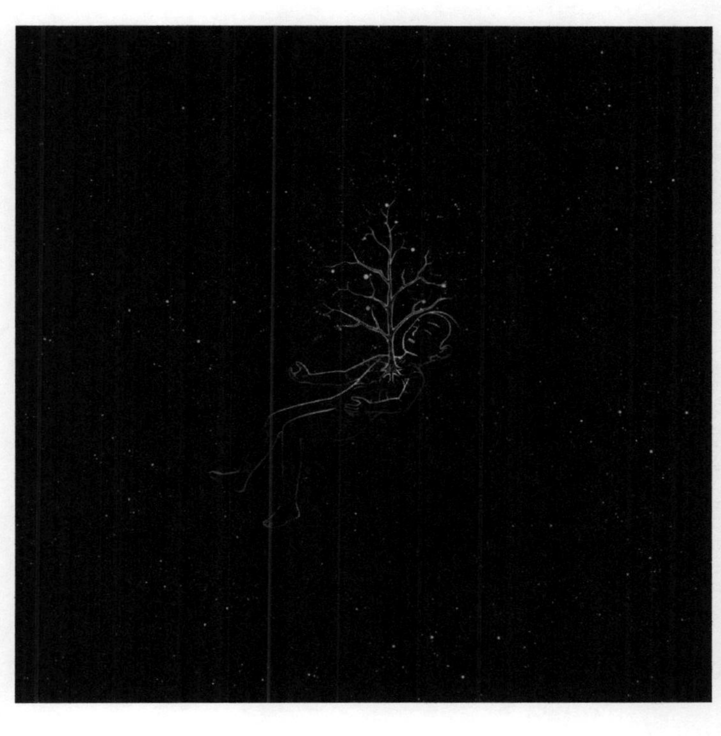

III
Soulful Rebirth

- I was never beautifully broken before.

Inside I died; I couldn't see myself in pain, struggling to break free to help myself. I had to shatter from inside to mould the collage of my inner child again, to unlearn so many conditionings and to learn new unspoken language of life which beholds softness, flexibility, tenderness, kindness; which encourages a soul to feel the purity of empathy, which gives the courage to know the unknown me, which nourishes your soul to have a positive perception about life throughout and through all. This feeling which generated deep down within the core of my soul and living gladly and gratefully with It and breathing with it every moment indeed is a REBIRTH in this one lifetime.

I didn't know I'll be able to live alively in this life again. Today I really feel that I'm blessed with love and goodness in life. Life is not always about wrong or right. Life is beyond these barriers for me. If you look through my vision about what life is, it's about the connection which I feel with my inner conscience.

The good and beauty of this life course should not be blocked by my unwanted mental and emotional toxicity, my soul should be love marked by my transparent and truthful words. Today my life is very dear to me, every moment of it. I hold it deeply very close to my heart. I live joyfully in this moment. I don't know I'll be breathing in the next moment or not, so I live through it, with it, all of it. The source of joy, happiness resides within me. Whatever life is, it is now. One promise I made to myself is that I will be there for myself soulfully. I'll never escape or abandon my soul again.

Being worried about what is going to happen is never going to let me feel content or as one within myself. I don't miss my inner child today, in this NOW. Allowing myself to know the unknown me and understanding its deepest depths, beyond fears of losing myself and being broken, lovingly, caringly which nourishes my beating heart is the sweetest acknowledgement that I feel today

I can feel content within myself only by sharing it all. This rebirth is not a conspiracy against the universe. It's the soulfulness which imbibes life and aligns each and every element for a greater cause.

> *Doors of gold, never sold,*
> *To a soul who didn't unfold.*
> *May it far, may it near,*
> *Though! Doors of gold are here.*
> *If you cry, if you see,*
> *It seems so clear*
> *When you are free.*
> *Against the flow, nothing ever grows,*
> *With it, it always shows.*
> *Blessed to have none,*
> *blessed to have all,*

The shades are deeper,
In autumn and fall.

IV
Little Things

- Time and tide has all the answers if a soul can truly observe and listen.

Waves have a deep level of sacrifice and let go. They know they have to crash at shore but still, they unconditionally keep on loving their colourful soul. Sacrificing without regretting over it, letting go of the unchangeable past in life, accepting my flaws, my strengths completely, accepting the process for all transformations in life – make a difference and awareness of the totality of my reality gifts me the vision of gratefulness about little things.

The sounds of the waves never fade, one who embraces with a warm heart can feel it within, and it sits in a corner of your heart which you thought was broken but was never broken though mended by the purity of the sound of the wave. How do you feel when you see an ocean full of unknown mysteries and yet it's so soothing and calm to your beloved soul? That little you who was lost in the nowhere land of past, lively sees itself and starts to love the heart again today, only by drowning without this fear of being lost and losing again.

For me, my flaws and strengths of mine are beautiful and gorgeous. I don't have any longing for cosmetic beauty. It's all about what I am inside, it depends on which element I am choosing for my soul and what I am willingly feeding my mind altogether. How am I rewiring my alignment and how much resilience is engraved in my dedication. My flaws and strengths give me the courage to be me wherever I flow, in whichever state or phase I am in. It doesn't take much. It only takes to not to give in to any negativity in any situation or circumstance. Accepting the wholeness of little things and allowing myself to be with the flexible alignment or direction of life.

Feeling the gravity, feeling the nature with my inner eye, feeling the elements of life, feeling the noises and the silence, feeling the bliss and the chaos, feeling the warmth of being alive, feeling the little things everywhere, every moment, every day – it's a privilege to be a part of this universe and to be the vessel to contain all the universe within me.

A Lovely haze with mountain dew it seems like the glory
As we knew
Just a thought
Which sees through an eyeful view?
A reason to embrace, a reason to sow
Bows down in front of the road
Silence of word which never showed,
That's The Grace which beholds...

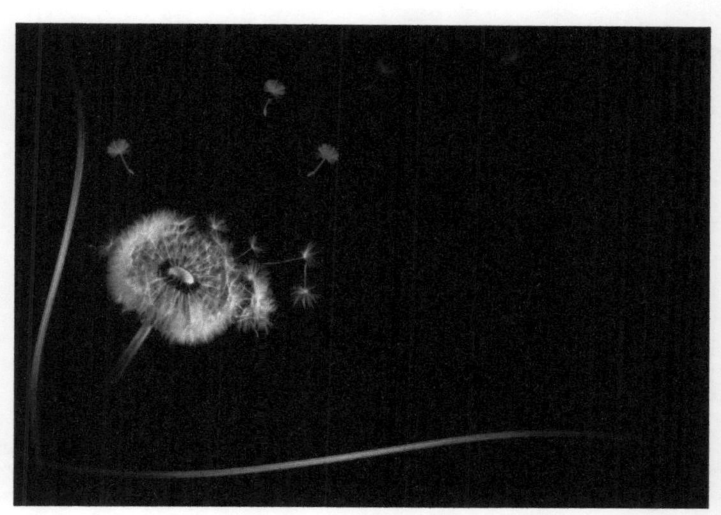

V
Becoming – Denial of being

Being my wholeness and becoming me – there is a difference between these two. Me has an 'I' embedded to it whereas wholeness is being total in real. The genuine is never very fond of becoming. It always loves to be in its whole version. No matter how much I try I always falter between these two.

Whenever I am going through some different phase of my life or some difficult situation, whenever some change is taking place, it is evident that my 'I' element will get irritated by every means. Most of the time I forget that we all thrive in energy because we believe in visibility so much. And therefore most deep, priceless elements go missing from our being. In both cases the actions we take we make ourselves according to that mould. Our process of being in accordance with the conscience shapes us. And one realization I had while effortlessly connecting with my own conscience – that in each and every turn of my life I will be pushed to the extreme limit, I'll be tested for my endurance, tolerance, kindness, love, compassion, empathy, absurdity, transparency and above all faith and believe over my being, my existence, trust over the supreme most energy and vibration of this universe.

'SWAYAM' – this is a Sanskrit word, which means self. A self only can be in the being when oneself is teachable in every moment of its entire life. No room for accommodating I or ego or becoming or looking through fragmented disrupted vision. This is entirely polluted by lustful false imagery or mirage. Worrying and bothering about seeking self also pushes us towards self-destruction. The only thing is being at peace with self and nourishing and exploring it lovingly with care aligns our elements and the need of becoming dissolves in the vast ocean of life.

Wanting more while having all, degrades the texture and essence of consciousness which gives birth to regret, sorrow and grief. I have been through that deviated path, now I am slowly returning to the 'SWAYAM' – my true self, without any veil, without having an illusion about myself, without keeping conditions to accept the wholeness of life, without becoming. The state of being.

The dawn always calls upon the dusk
There is an eternal light
Inside all of us.
So rise, rise above all
And see yourself standing with you
Embracing all.
Look inside of your sight
It feels so beautiful.
The aura of being,
It's all that cures...

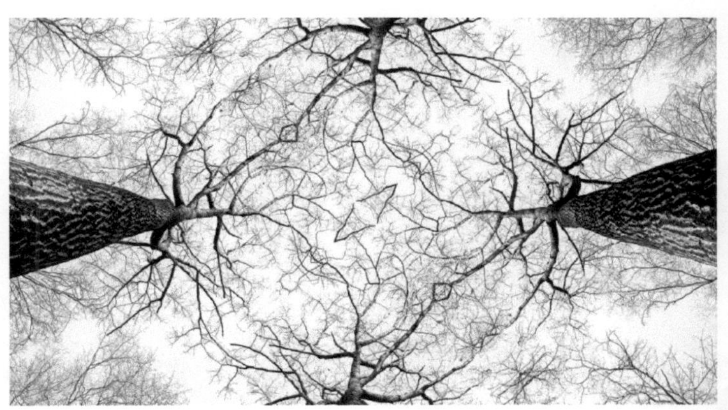

VI
Let it

All I used to ask was why me all the time? Be it the process, be it the path, and be it the way of happening- all matters in this life; the words, the meanings of it, the way of saying and seeing things, the going and coming- all matters in this one life.

Love, betrayal, response, reaction, reaching, stepping back, silence, screaming, running, pausing - all count in being wiser in our thoughts. By not becoming; we walk in the path of being. Gradual consistency vs. everyday resilience, every component nourishes us throughout. We judge the doings of us, the doing of others, the doing of all, does that count in being wiser!

Ferocious keeping vs. probable reasoning can mend the pieces according to the actual truth beyond all judgements. We need to think again on these two perceptions- 'am I free by drowning into the life stream' or have I saved myself by taking the diverted route, not by merging my entire self into the lifestream, by escaping some by embracing some'

We create the society as we want to see it, not the actual all of it. And above all, we all are one society within ourselves. It's a mirage in which we live. How can it be frictionless to live only with mirages of life and not the actual of it?

We plant the seed of superficial, vague mirages within us and nourish it so caringly without even realizing that shallow can never be the way of life.

Have we ever tried to look at our anatomy of body and brain in detail? Have we ever thoroughly looked at the structure of it, that how deep detailing is present in us? Or have we ever felt the connection with the universe! Which is actually very deep?

Shallow living builds a weak root for life. So when needed we can barely hold onto that root to our inner being or conscience.

Nothing, no being has an image or no image to keep. We all have a form only to be formless from within, without any rigidity like shapeless water, very flexible towards life, towards our self.

No entity can be flawless. So hereby today I declare to myself to explore all of my beings. By not claiming to know everything all the time, by letting my soul open to all, which is life.

VII
Being thoughtful (Reality)

Why reasons are so questionable sometimes? Did we forget to dive deeper within? Or does it takes too much from us to deal with the reality? Why is it not enough for the human race that we are alive still? Why can't we be free completely within a moment? Why always our external indulgence forces us to see the shades of grey only?

When believing became a lie in this glamour, shadowed world! Then by knowing what truth is, why can't we stop seeking the truth and be within it only?

Isn't it beautiful to see through us! We are really about nothing and solemnly NOTHING is all about us. Be within or be without, if we do not possess we all are free from the known. Nothing matters but nothing is the only element of living that resides within. As the inner child knows when all are embraced life blossoms in between every piece in the collage of life.

Dying within oneself is either resurrection of life within or selfishly abandoning our aura. It's a matter of fact that we all mostly choose the second option. The first option sounds melancholy. But it only takes the deepest harmony to synchronise with the melancholy of our life, our soul never asks for more than that. The synchronicity of melancholy with harmony within, says it all for us to the external world through the reflection of our aura. It is always a voyage within. It is all the journey which we walk with the soulful solitude synchronised with the source, its 'US'. It is always the silence that unconditionally fills the emptiness.

The Convergence
Some parts of the lexicon of life are real, gentle,
some parts are harsh.
The combination of harsh and polite is very clear in this
division.
Everything that has gone away comes back in a new
outfit,
Like the arrival of autumn,
Like the outfit of the new moon,
As if the sunny sky is painted like red vermilion.
In the embrace of the life lexicon of one sky,
How many unspoken promises want to touch the soul
with both hands?
Like the migrant returned to his home in the late
afternoon,
He was filled with peace.
These words, therefore, come in quiet and tell the story,
Saying that
The words meet in silence today
The beginning of the convergence...

VIII
Hiraeth

I used to believe that I belong to someone, someplace- that I belong to something in this world. But the journey of longing is always nostalgically inward.

Today I really do believe that I belong to my own conscience, myself. I belong to me. I'm still walking on that path to feeling one within with myself, with all of me.

This hiraeth calls upon that wiseness, that wisdom which is gifted to humanity. It summons the self-betrayal, the self-hatred, the self conning. We all are masters of these all patterns. Knowingly or unknowingly we keep on breaking ourselves into immoral pieces which hold no value for us at the end of this savage process, it leaves us with an unworthy essence for us and our being. So many questions appear at that time but the burden of defeat is so heavy that our conscience cannot move out of that vicious zone.

After so many incidents in my life, finally, I started the process to be my hiraeth. Started to feel a very deep longing for my being within, where I feel home.

I truly feel that if I love myself, my soul and all of my being. Ill unconditionally embrace the ocean which I hold within- no matter what form or what phase it is in! A moon also has its scars and changing phases but when it shines it brightens a dark path.

This change within is me, deep scars are me which are enchanted today, the healing pain is mine, the joyous is me, the transformation is me- today I feel the urge to connect with every piece of mine, to be whole again. Started embracing all the sunshine and rain of life-the 'all of me', so that I can make peace with another soul, not chaos.

Only by embracing all my broken pieces with love and affection, I am building a home inside my heart full of bliss, space and contentment. Where a sense of completeness I feel within myself. It feels so cosy, calm, and serene to be connected with my entire being. By being on this journey with myself I feel the oneness with my beloved universe.

Now I summon the dark

Within which I dwell.

To feel the moon rays

Over the dark shadows,

Let the pure within bloom

Like lavender in chaos.

Let the longing call me silently in the storm

Let the hiraeth be me for my soul

As eternal and so on...

IX
The Journey continues...

Occurring moments are relative, spoken words are relative, thoughts are relative, past, present, future is relative. Somewhere listening, somewhere seeing, somewhere sounding, somewhere reminiscing

Relativity changes form with time.

Depending on the person and the thinking, the relative journey will be marked or questioned. Relativity depends on the development of human attitude, thinking and humanity.

Everything in this journey from birth to death is relative in these present course above all relative conditions. Because the creation, change and destruction are above relatives, everywhere and this journey is immersed in it throughout.

There, beneath shallow resides my soul which is blooming out of darkness, seeing the light for the first time. An ocean is storming to breakthrough. Silence is the strongest voice that is heard by the hearts either shallow or deep. This twister, roller coaster of life is easy. Becomes easy only with consideration and depth of acceptance. So, therefore, living a soulful smile and tasting a drop of tear is very worthy to be the light. These are the ornaments supreme most gifted us, these are the gifts of life. Valuing all beings all. It's the journey of life.

There lays a mystic beneath the soul, which sounds like rain, it whispers like a calm blowing wind. My beloved has an essence of charm which dives deep inside the eyes and feels the stillness in a storm. So calm and so blissful. An ecstatic motion of oneness. We behold an ocean inside. A world within so serene, so pure.

I could see the reflection of my inner soul inside the transparent teardrops of mine. The more grey my past became, the more I could distinguish between the colours of life, the more I dived deeper within the moments, within the shades of past and present the uncertain future seemed so blissful and serene because it is what it is, nothing more, nothing less. Without imposing an assumed image to it or without looking at it with a predefined fake realistic notion we can feel the essence of reality.

In this present, I can connect from the core of my soul. It feels like my soul is my beloved and I am unconditionally and endlessly falling in love with it and rising from the ashes like a phoenix. It is not a war within anymore. It filled up with serene silence, blissful solitude, non-provoking emptiness, not fearing the fears anymore, rudimental life in each and every moment, nurturing and exploring all gifted aspects of it. Keeping the space externally and internally to be the flexibility to explore beyond possessing and wanting. Being grateful without any barrier or condition towards the wholeness, towards all, towards being one within, with the universe.

The journey continues
The journey of oneness
Within...
> *Strings are not entangled anymore together*
> *It is beyond every attachment.*
> *Togetherness which we feel today*
> *It's the oneness, as a whole.*
> *Defeated times and again*
> *Yet undefeated in life.*
> *The deepest conscience*
> *Slowly fluttering their wings*
> *Breaking free*
> *Can see the change as a sign.*
> *Pain is growing,*
> *And the transformations also,*
> *Seems so lovely as life sows.*
> *The oneness is destined together,*
> *It's the journey of metamorphosis...*

X

Mirrors

(1)
Visiting my reflections for a while
Staying up to make it smiles.
It seems same all the time
Gloomy, sad
Painted in grief and saturnine.
It doesn't sound similar to me anymore
The veil is dark
Can't see through the door.

A rotten reflection says it all
Why so distant from the call?
It says can't you hear the chime! Of your own?
Fearful about what! This you is you at all?
Look through me; sing to your soul,
I'll see again, will go through it all.

This healing pain
It is worthy of my soul...

(2)
How deep is the ocean of madness?
How crystal a vision can be?
How impeccable I am with my soul?
How much it takes to consider 'ME"?

SHINY

Is it real joy which we look for?
Does seeking always give an answer?

How much true is a truth?
How much false is false?
Why in silence we feel the chaos?
Why a whole seems fragmented in grief?

Is it worthy to forget myself?
Is it worthy to be fooled by my seeing?
I don't know anything
That is, above all
Life is a valley of meadow on sheen...

9 781684 872596

Printed by Libri Plureos GmbH in Hamburg,
Germany